Drawing For Beginners:

The Ultimate Drawing Art, Sketching, Pencil Drawing Techniques, Exercises and Lessons Guide

By

Angela Pierce

Table of Contents

Drawing For Beginners: The Ultimate Drawing Art, Sketching, Pencil Drawing Techniques, Exercises and Lessons Guide

By Angela Pierce

First Published, 2015

Printed in the United States of America

Introduction

There are thousands of drawing related careers in the market. The fact that printers and digital photo editing tools are taking over the market does not mean that a fine artist with a set of pencils is good for nothing. Actually, if you can perfect the art, your sketches and paintings will always fetch a better price than print set ones. A touch of taste that goes into every hand painting. Mastering your technique in time could put you somewhere, either locally or internationally.

The most impressive thing about drawing and painting is you do not have to be formally employed to work. You can do it as a side job, or take it as a full job from your home studio. Whatever path you chose, what matter is how well you can draw. Getting the basics perfect could be the only firm foundation you need to bring out the artist in you.

Chapter 1. Basic Drawing Techniques

There is more to drawing than putting pencil to paper. Hatching, cross-hatching, stipping, scumbling, back and forth stroke and coming up with a clear outline are crucial techniques of drawing that every artist should get familiar with. These techniques give your image life and allow the audience mind to wonder. In that case, a good artist should be inclined to follow all these techniques to the latter.

Creating an outline for your drawing is essential. Any complete drawing has to have two outlines, with the first being lighter than the next. A lighter outline is necessary when creating basic shapes that make up the image. While a heavy outline may be used to make up the edges of your drawing. The technique is simple; do not press your pencil too hard on your paper.

You do not want to make it too difficult to erase your image when the image does not come out the way you want. Using different types of pencils, you can come up with a variety of lines. On the other hand, you can also come up with various types of line values and thickness depending on the way you hold the pencil.

Using the sides of your pencil will definitely get thicker lines, whereas when you use the front part of your pencil you will get thin lines.

The second techniques in drawing are hatching and crosshatching. For the most part, hatching technique is used to offer a shading effect on your object. Preferably, the lines should be drawn following one direction to define them better. On the other hand, crosshatching makes your image look more real. To come up with crosshatching line, first draw hatching lines heading in one direction. Then cross over these lines in the opposite direction.

Another handy technique you can apply is the circular technique. This technique is particularly important when it comes to shading of your image. In that case, you have to move your pencil in a swirling motion to keep the swirls and circles as close together as you can.

You can also make your image look realistic by adding smooth shading lines. These lines can be created in a manner of ways. First, you can use the side of your pencil to create smooth strokes that are close together. Start with a harder pencil as you move on to a softer one. Do not separate your lines too much since that will only make your image have a rough look.

It takes time to become better in drawing. The techniques might seem simple but they are really a painstaking procedure. Master each step as you advance form a beginner to get a chance to burgeon as an artist. Be yourself as an artist. Do not follow trends that are not you. Do not be scared to think outside the box since you will only lock yourself in ideas that have already been explored. Come up with a trend and let it guide other artists to come up with their own style.

Chapter 2. Good Drawing Principles

Great artists need a grounding that they can build on to acquire self-actualization. Coupled with determination and impetus, achieving immeasurable success is inevitable. Being unique and innovative is a start, but there is more to it. Perhaps the most important trait an artist should have is a creative mind.

As times change, so does trends. In that case, a good artist should be able to adapt to come up with his own ideas that are very different from what other artists are offering. While creativity is a gift, it can also be nurtured. A good artist should release something new every single time to keep the audience coming back for more.

Besides that, a good artist should be aware of what the audience wants. Take time to know what your audience interests and make advancements from there. This helps to stick to a particular frame of work while making improvements on what exists. Well, occasionally you can switch just to surprise your audience, which is beneficial for the hype.

Aside from this, a good artist should have an infatuation for what he does. There is so little that can be done when there is no muse. A good artist has strong feelings for what he does. He will not give up for anything. On that note, a good artist has to have an inherent passion for what he does to ensure that the love never dies.

Furthermore, an artist should be business minded. Apart from pursuing a dream, art is a source of livelihood. For that reason, it should be approached with a high level of seriousness. A good artist can market his work and earn a living out of it. If an artist has another full-time job he has set life on, this might interfere with his ability to burgeon in the niche. As a result, an artist should rely on one niche if he is to remain focused on what he truly wants in life.

A great artist must have a keen eye on a creating a masterpiece. It is one thing to come up with a good piece, but it is something else to create an acceptable work of art. Therefore, an artist should consider the audience. Nothing should be undervalued when it comes to quality.

Good artists spend most of their time with people who share the similar interests with the ones they have. Irrespective of the niche, surrounding yourself with negative energy will always bring down your attempts of flourishing. Therefore, a good artist should know what he or she wants. Moreover, s great artist must be vigilant and ready to pursue what he wants in his career. Nothing should hold your efforts back to improve on any success they have recently achieved.

Lastly, a good artist should be steadfast. There is no straight path in becoming a great artist. Perhaps the rise and fall is what makes success even sweeter. Resilience is just part of being a maestro.

Chapter 3. Understanding The Drawing Perspectives

Perspective refer to a way of capturing visual images on a flat surface like that of a plain piece of paper but in form of a drawing. A perspective is evident when the following two characteristics are visible. One, the farther an observer is from an object, the smaller the object becomes. Two, the dimensions of the object along the line of sight are shorter than they are across the line of sight. There are so many types of perspectives but the most commonly known are one-, two- and three-point. These names are as such because of the number of points that seem to disappear in the actual drawing.

One-point perspective

A drawing is categorized as one-point perspective when only one single vanishing point is seen on the horizon line. Such images are those of the likes of roads, railways tracks, hallways or such buildings that are seen as if the front most part is directly facing the person viewing the object. Parallel or perpendicular lines to the viewer's line of sight converge at one vanishing point hence the name one-point perspective.

Drawing in this perspective is the easiest and a fun way to introduce your plain looking drawing to appear in 2D of 3D dimensional images. As simple as having one vanishing point, your angles, shapes and horizon does not need much but just to disappear right into the same vanishing point.

Two-point perspective

Similar to one-point perspective, two-point perspective holds the same idea but slightly deviating a little bit. Two vanishing points disappear into the horizon line. Two-point perspective can be applied in drawing the same object just like it was done with one-point perspective but this time round they are rotated. An example is given by looking at a house from the point of view of a corner. One wall would appear to head towards one vanishing point while the other one to the opposite vanishing point.

In addition to the single vanishing point in the one-point dimension, two point dimension needs an additional vanishing point. Two parallel vanishing points are made to appear each into a well-known point of vanish. When drawing your shapes, angles and horizon, make sure that you draw your vanishing lines in correspondence to the right vanishing point. Although it is a bit complex, you can draw 3D effects to look just perfect.

Three-point perspective

Three-Point Perspective is a bit different from the other two types of perspectives. It is evident in buildings seen from above or below because the vanishing point is in the high space or in underground depending on how the viewer looks at the building. The two vanishing points from the two-point perspective are made to appear as if they are headed for the ground or for the sky. Three-point perspective is made when the perspective is a Cartesian scene view but in that particular situation where the picture plane is not in the parallel direction as that of any of the scenes three axes. Every vanishing point is in correspondence with one of the three axes available in the scene.

In order to create three-point perspective, you need the mastery of both one-point and two-point perspectives. It could get more complicated if you do not know where to join or which vanishing points to make your vanishing lines disappear to. The only extra addition you will have to make is make you drawing a tall building and choose to view it either from above or below. Always remember that the vanishing points will always be below the ground or in the high space depending on where the viewer makes his observation.

Chapter 4. Sketching Tips

Trees

The first step and one that is simple would be to draw an ace of cards that in essence would be drawing three circles with a triangle as the base. This will act as your framework. It is the blue print that guides you to drawing your tree. The lines of the circles and triangle should be as faint as possible. You will then be required to sketch out the branches and the trunk. The trunk will follow the line of the triangle while the branches will occupy the circles. Next would be to sketch the outline of the branches. At this point, some branches may have to be covered.

The sunlight will then have to be brought in. decide on which side you want the sun to be situated. That would mean that the opposite side of the tree will have to be shed with shadows of the trunk, branches and leaves. Drawing individual leaves will be too hectic and would look unreal. Going with the shadings is the best way to go about it. The bottom line where the trunk meets the ground has to be done away with as it looks like the trunk is just floating on top of the ground.

Rocks

The first step is to draw the outlines of your rock(s). We then draw the major shadows by use of lines. The lines help to curve the planes of the rock. These are the angled surfaces of a rock. They help in outlining the real volume of the rock. Cracks can also be used to show the planes. The next step would be to highlight the wedges of the rocks. When added, it gives more life to your rocks. Cracks are always part of many rocks. They also help in showing the planes. You only have to ensure that you change the angle of the crack whenever you move from one plane to the next.

The last step will include addition of texture. This can be done by making a combination of small scratches and dots. Depending on where you want your sunlight to be, you will have to deepen the shadows on the opposite side of the sun. The shadows are also to be added at the base of the rocks to give them weight. The texture in the shadow at the base is to indicate grass. With that, your drawing will be more than complete and looking awesome.

First things to be drawn before anything else are the guides for the body and the head. You will the follow with the facial guidelines. In this case we shall be drawing a puppy, therefore, you can outline its nose and finish up the head by adding the ears and some little bit of hair in between them. The big friendly eyes should follow next in addition to the nose and mouth. A happy pappy will be great. A sad one may turn out to be a headache. As for the body, you will start with the front legs and paws then move to the hind legs. Its curly tail will come in last among the features. You could add some bit of fur if you please.

By now you should have a complete puppy. Erasing of the guidelines and making any necessary corrections will follow before you start thinking of giving it paint. That should be all. However, other animals may not be as easy as the puppy because they may come with more defined features. However, they all follow the same guideline. Difference in size does not mean that they have different approaches to drawing them. It may just take you more time to complete.

There are two methods you can use to draw car. You can either do free hand or use the grid method. In the free hand method, you may begin with the baseline then draw the wheels. Makes sure they are spaced correctly. The rooflines can then be made using large pencil strokes. The next step would be to outline the shadows of the door panels. In case you find it hard to draw curved lines you can simply take it one short and quick stroke at a time. Finish up with the bottom and the nose details.

With the grid method, all you have to do is draw a grid the size in length and height of the car you want to draw. You can then draw the car square by square till it is complete. From here you will have to erase the grid. Between the two methods, the free hand is easier and faster but the grid method is more accurate. You can now start shading the car. From the roof, the body, the wheels all the way to the interior. The outer edges should be made a little darker. The tyres should have a darker outer part and the rims a bit lighter. The shadow beneath the car should not miss.

People

Drawing people can pose a big challenge. The symmetry of the face and shape of the body can be very hard especially if you are still trying to sharpen your skills. The first thing to do would be to simplify a person's major shapes. If you are referencing from a picture, you can draw the shapes on the picture before you start sketching. Circling these parts such as the nose, eyes, cheeks, forehead, and the back head is akin to breaking everything down. Once you outline the shapes that make up the structure of the face or body, you will have a better understanding of the proportions and distance between features.

When you start to sketch, you should start with the head going downwards. You can simply start by drawing a shape that is similar to the head. You will then proceed to the neck. As for the shoulders, you can draw a line perpendicular to the base of the neck. Its distance should be about 2 to 3 head widths and followed by small circles at the end of the lines. Below them would be oval shapes that will form the upper arms. This goes on until when you have a full body after which you start sketching the individual's face and body. The shapes only act as your guideline.

Chapter 5. The Art of Arranging Items

Drawing is an art. Therefore, it is only natural that it embodies the all the things that make up an art. From the planning all the way to the final product, a drawing needs to be given all the attention it requires. When drawing, there is always a format that one is advised to follow. There is an arrangement of things. The items drawn do not just fall into place. You have to arrange them properly. Whether it is in the imagination of the artist or whether they are drawing from a set of things that have been displayed for them, the arrangement has to take a certain order.

Coming up with the group

You have to select the items you want to draw beforehand. You have to come up with the criteria for selecting the items. The items may be diverse but should have a thing or the other I common. It could be stationery, grocery, or even utensils. Gather as many as you can and set them up on a table.

Before arranging the objects, you have to come up with the principle or the primary object and the secondary objects. These two will determine the how the items will be arranged. The primary object acts as the leader of the group. The first thing to be considered will be if you want the items to form any figure when they are arranged. It has to be artistic in every way.

The principal object has to be placed centrally where it is easily visible. It does not have to be at the center. Arrangement of the other items will then follow next. Try not to place them in a straight line with the principle object. Their axis should not all be upright or horizontal. They should be organized and form a pattern that is not too obvious. In terms of impression, the appearance should be that of objects at rest.

Some of the objects should be partially hidden from the others. In case the objects appear to be of the same height when you draw them, you will have to change them. Whatever the case, the arrangement should be able to form a great artistic composition.

The items should be of a wide variety. The diversification will be able to portray unity when they are arranged together. You can have some objects arranged far back than others. This brings the aspect of distance into the picture and it in turn portrays the feeling of freedom. This is what one is supposed to feel when they are drawing the items. Thinking of the items as little beings will be able to help a lot in generating ideas of how to arrange them.

The aspect of great composition is to give the drawing life, to make it not just appealing but informative too. A good arrangement is what makes a picture great. It is just like when drawing of a portrait. The person being drawn has to embody certain characteristics to make the drawing a masterpiece.

Chapter 6. How to Tell a Story Through a Painting

Words are to a writer what a paint brush is to an artist. Pictures may be worth a thousand words but paintings are worth a million stories. Ever since the time immemorial, there have come artists who have left their mark in the world courtesy of the great master pieces they left behind. Paintings have always been used as a way of telling stories. As an artist, mastering this art of communicating to your audience through your drawings marks the beginning of your maturity as an artist. It may not necessarily be your own story. It could be tales of others or occurrences in history.

Think of a story line

This is the tale that you want to communicate to the people. It is the message that you wish to relay out there to the masses. It could be one story about the past or the present or it could be more than one story in a single painting. There has to be a general theme about the story you want to tell. This would be the most outstanding feature on the painting. It would be the first thing that catches the eye when one throws one glance at the painting. This may vary from culture of a people, immorality, violence, or just history. Once you have a story in mind then you have to start thinking of the ways you will tell it. You should be able to tell it in the best way possible.

The characters of the story

A story has to have characters or subjects. The characters are the main protagonists of the story. The story revolves around him/her or them. This protagonist may be a man, an animal, or even an area. By having a subject, the artist will be able to tell his story in relation to the subject.

For instance, a painting that shows Nelson Mandela being arrested by white officers to be taken to prison amid chaos by his supporters will tell the story of a man who is probably loved by his people. It will also tell the story of a society facing oppression. It will tell us a lot of things about the man and the moment.

The environment

The surrounding environment is always one with the story being told. This is where the color schemes to be used come into play. Depending on the story being told, the color will be able to communicate the mood at that single moment.

Dark colors could go with a somber mood while bright colors may be used to express the joy and warmth. The environment will also be able to tell you a lot about the people of the area and the activities they are involved in. Their cultural can also be portrayed from the environment or setting of the painting.

Paintings have always and will always tell stories for a long time. It is the one form of art that communicates without having to utter a single word. You just have to watch and listen to the whispers from the painting.

Chapter 7. Drawing Exercises

Drawing straight exercise

Some things in nature appear to be made of straight lines, or perfect curves. Trying to replicate these with a ruler, however, would result into perfect unnatural straight lines. How do you beat this? By using this simple exercise to drawing straight.

- Instead of drawing one long piece, draw your shapes using small short lines joined up

- The more the curve the shorter the lines to use

- Once you are done with the short outline, join them together with soft strokes of the pencil

- Remember to keep your hand light and easy, drawing should be fun, not a task.

Settling the nerve exercise

Most beginner artists tend to be nervous. As a result, their hands will shake leading to irregular movement of the pencil. Here are a couple of tricks to calm your hand and get your groove on

- Get a pencil, a sharp one, and a sketchpad and begin drawing shapes like circles or rectangles while shaking your hand voluntarily

- Start making your hand steady without increasing the pressure on the paper with your pencil

- Repeat the process for new shapes until you can draw steadily with your palm lying firmly on the paper and only using your fingers to move the pencil

- Once you have perfected this, you can lift off your hand from the paper and try steadying your arm

- You should be repeating this before drawing until you are steady enough to jump straight in

Sketch practice

While most beginners will try to make perfect from the word go, there is a lot about natural movement and drawing in general you have to learn gradually. The natural movement of the hand is key to getting your drawing right. Sketch as many things as you can. From boxes, people, dogs to your TV screen. Don't worry of the outcome, just concentrate on stilling your arm and making the lines as regular as possible.

Following a tutorial practice

If you are to use tutorials in sketching, it does you no good to replicate what is on offer. Here is an exercise that will jog your mind.

Try changing sizes whilst maintaining perspectives, this will make you understand perspective drawing better

Put on additional features to tutorials to invent your own drawing. This will help you practice on object placement.

Use regular shapes, for instance circles to get your proportions right.

For instance, two ovals out of phase by 90 degrees will help you draw a manly face better.

Two circles, a small one to the front and a bigger one at the back and slightly to the side will help you get a dog's muzzle perspective right.

- Draw a small circle at the centre of the page

- Draw two lines diverging from the circle's centre at a 30-degree angle. Draw another bigger circle touching the diverging lines

- You have your perspective. Remember to keep the circles and diverging lines light, as they are not part of the final sketch

Conclusion

Art, sometimes, is all about creativity. However, being creative without the right skills to output these ideas would be futile. Any good artist has a firm foundational knowledge of all the sketching concepts. While covering these concepts in a single sitting would be next to impossible, heightening your skills by practicing on the most basic drawing tasks could be the very practice you need to get better by the day.

Remember that it is the most basic drawing skills and concepts that when put together result into something awesome and amazing. After mastering the basics, try applying your skills onto more complex drawing jobs. For instance, instead of drawing a simple cartoon without hair, try mixing your skill of drawing wigs with drawing the cartoon. Give it some hair. If this works, use your object placement and perspective skills to add more objects into the drawing. Experimenting and being gradual is the perfect way to combining tutorials with your own skill in your quest to being a perfect artist.

Thank You Page

I want to personally thank you for reading my book. I hope you found information in this book useful and I would be very grateful if you could leave your honest review about this book. I certainly want to thank you in advance for doing this.

If you have the time, you can check my other books too.